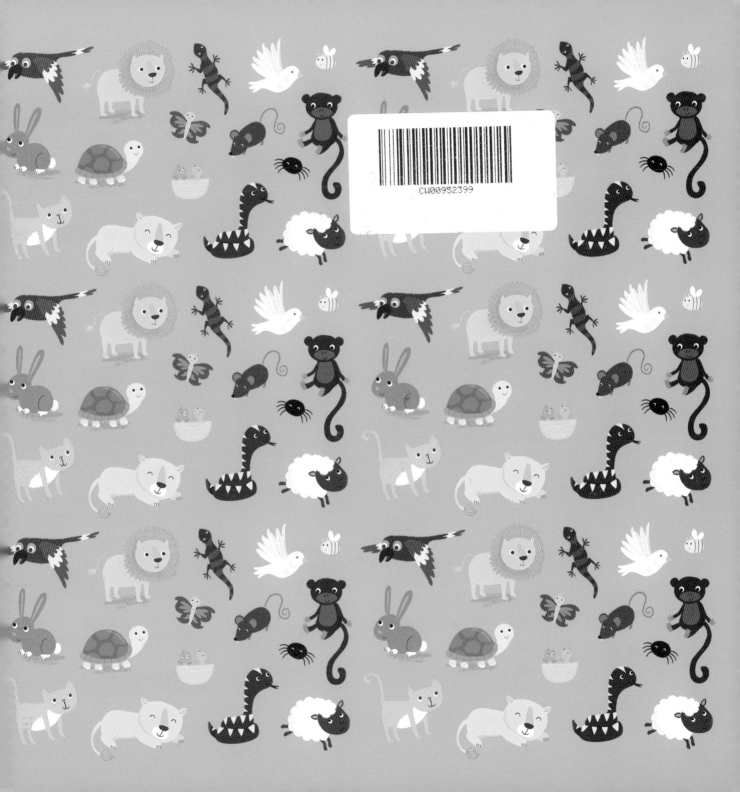

Text by Julia Stone
Illustrations copyright © 2015 Samantha Meredith
This edition copyright © 2019 Lion Hudson IP Limited

Published by
Lion Hudson Limited
Wilkinson House, Jordan Hill Business Park
Banbury Road, Oxford OX2 8DR, England
www.lionhudson.com

ISBN 978 0 7459 7832 1

First edition 2015

A catalogue record for this book is available from the British Library

Printed and bound in China, March 2019, LH54

I SPY
BIBLE

Written by Julia Stone

Illustrations by Samantha Meredith

LION
CHILDREN'S

Contents

In the beginning

In the beginning, the Bible says,
God made the world and everything
in it.

"I'm pleased," said God.
"It's very, very good."

Can you spot

 a parrot

a lion

 two rabbits

Eve

 five fruits

a lizard

Noah and the ark

God told Noah to build an ark.

"Take your family on the ark," said God, "and two of every kind of animal.

"I will keep you safe from a flood. Then you can start the world bright and new."

Can you spot

two tortoises

two monkeys

two pandas

two crocodiles

two tigers

Noah

Moses

God spoke to Moses.

"My people are sad, because they are slaves to a wicked king.

"I am choosing you to lead them to a land of their own.

"I will make a way through the sea so you can escape."

Can you spot

 five fish

a tambourine

 a boy holding a lamb

Moses

 a basket

a baby

David

Goliath was very tall and very fierce.
He had a sword and a spear
and a shield.

David was a shepherd boy.
He had a stick and a sling.

"God will help me beat you,"
said David.

He slung a stone.
Goliath fell down.

Can you spot

a vulture

a shield
bearer

four sheep

eight
shields

two
butterflies

Goliath's
helmet

Daniel

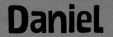

Daniel was in a deep, dark den. He was being punished by the emperor for saying his prayers.

God sent an angel into the den. The lions fell asleep.

God kept Daniel safe.

Can you spot

 two lion cubs

a pile of bones

 two spiders

the emperor

 three rats

two daddy lions

Baby Jesus

Here is the stable in Bethlehem.
Here are Joseph and Mary and
little baby Jesus.

Who else has come to see the baby?

Can you spot

 a hen and her chicks

a bright star

 a cat

Baby Jesus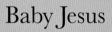

 a shepherd boy

an ox

Jesus in Galilee

On the hills of Galilee, Jesus was talking. "Love one another," he said. "Forgive one another. Then you will be God's children. God will always take care of you."

Can you spot

 a lunch basket

two boats

 two birds

six pink flowers

 four sheep

Jesus

Jesus' story of the lost sheep

The shepherd had spent all day looking for his lost sheep. He got home at sunset.

He called to his friends. "I found my lost sheep," he said. "Let's have a party."

God is like that shepherd, and God is happy when someone who was lost is found.

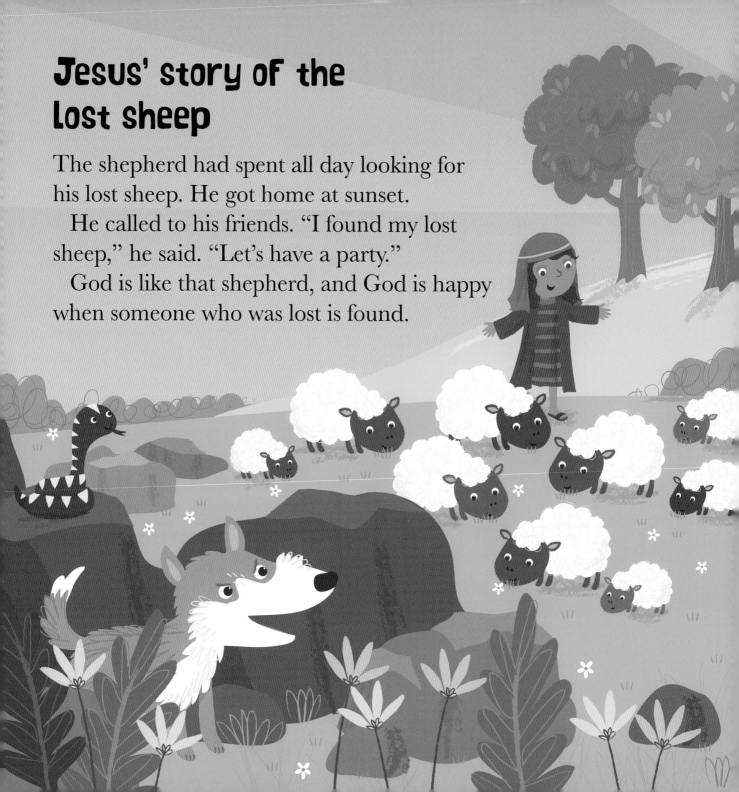

Can you spot

 a snake

a lost
sheep

 a jackal

a bear

 a wolf

the good
shepherd

Jesus' story of the great feast

A rich man was giving a party. The people he had invited didn't turn up.

He sent his servant to invite poor people. They came at once and were happy.

Can you spot

 four cats

a boy with a crutch

 a fish dish

six skittles

 five gold goblets

the rich man

Riding to Jerusalem

Jesus was riding to the big city of Jerusalem.
People cheered and waved palms.
"We want you to be our king!" they cried.
But Jesus had enemies. They frowned.

Can you spot

four children
waving palms

a musical pipe

two
Pharisees

two sheep

a donkey

Jesus

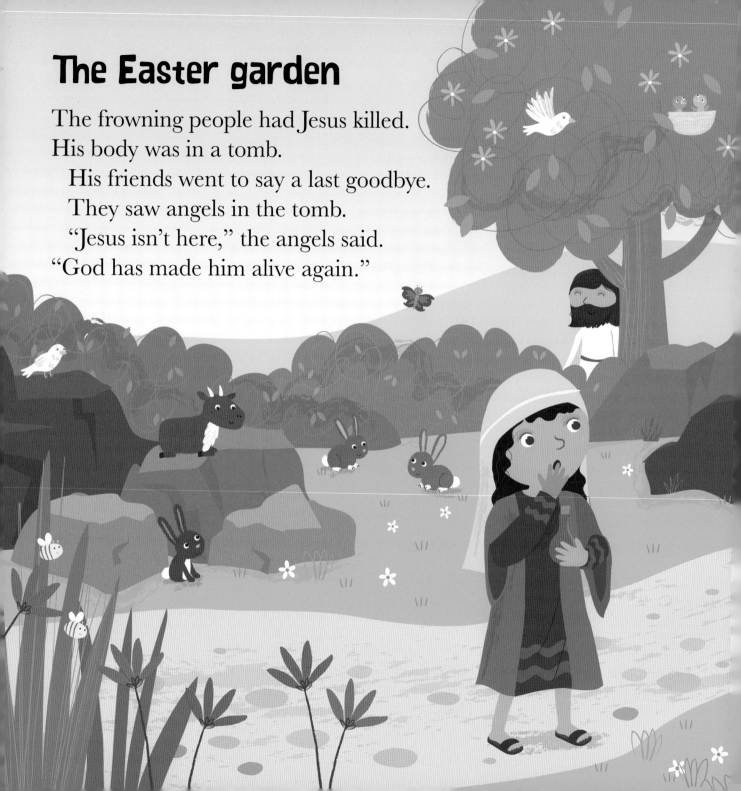

The Easter garden

The frowning people had Jesus killed.
His body was in a tomb.
   His friends went to say a last goodbye.
   They saw angels in the tomb.
   "Jesus isn't here," the angels said.
"God has made him alive again."

Can you spot

 three doves

three rabbits

 Mary Magdalene

tree in blossom

 a bird's nest

Jesus

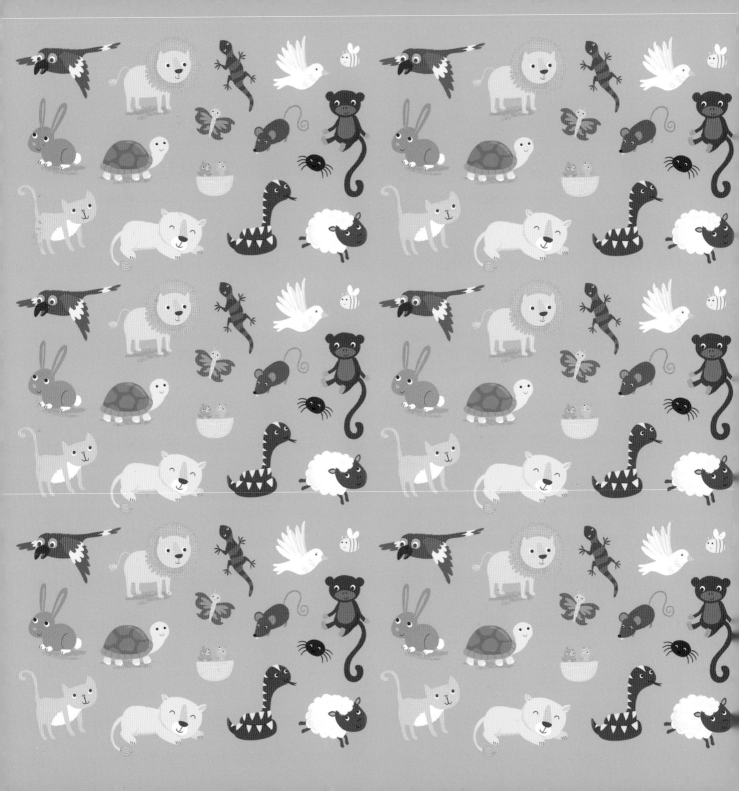